D0319565

Rubbish and Litter

Jen Green

WAYLAND

First published in 2009 by Wayland

Wayland
338 Euston Road
London NW1 3BH

Wayland Australia
Level 17/207 Kent Street
Sydney NSW 2000

Editor: Katie Powell
Designer: Elaine Wilkinson
Consultant: Kate Ruttle
Picture Researcher: Shelley Noronha
Photographer: Andy Crawford

British Library Cataloguing in Publication Data
Green, Jen
Rubbish and litter. - (Reduce, reuse, recycle!)
1. Recycling (Waste, etc.) - Juvenile literature 2. Waste minimization - Juvenile literature 3. Litter (Trash) - Juvenile literature
I. Title
363.7'288

ISBN: 978 0 7502 5714 5

Cover: Stockbyte/Photolibrary

1 Wayland Picture Library, 2 Altrendo Nature/Getty Images, 4 Ecoscene / photog, 5 Wayland Picture Library, 7 Banana Stock/jupiterimages/ImagePick, 8 & Cover Stockbyte/photolibrary.com, 9 Recycle Now, 10 Stockbyte/photolibrary.com, 11 Colin Seddon/Nature, 12 Wayland, 13 Altrendo Nature/Getty Images, 14 © Robert van der Hilst/CORBIS, 15 t, c, b ISTOCK,16 © Will & Deni McIntyre/CORBIS. 17 Wayland Picture Library, 18 Recycle Now, 19 © Don Mason/CORBIS, 20, 21 Wayland Picture Library, 22 Recycle Now, 23, 24, 25, 26, 27 Ecoscene / photog, 28 l & r Wayland, 29 r Wayland, 29 l & b Recycle Now

With thanks to RecycleNow.

The author and publisher would like to thank the following models: Sam Mears and Madhvi Paul.

Printed in China

Wayland is a division of Hachette Children's Books, an Hachette UK company.
www.hachette.co.uk

Contents

Words in **bold** can be found in the glossary.

The problem of waste

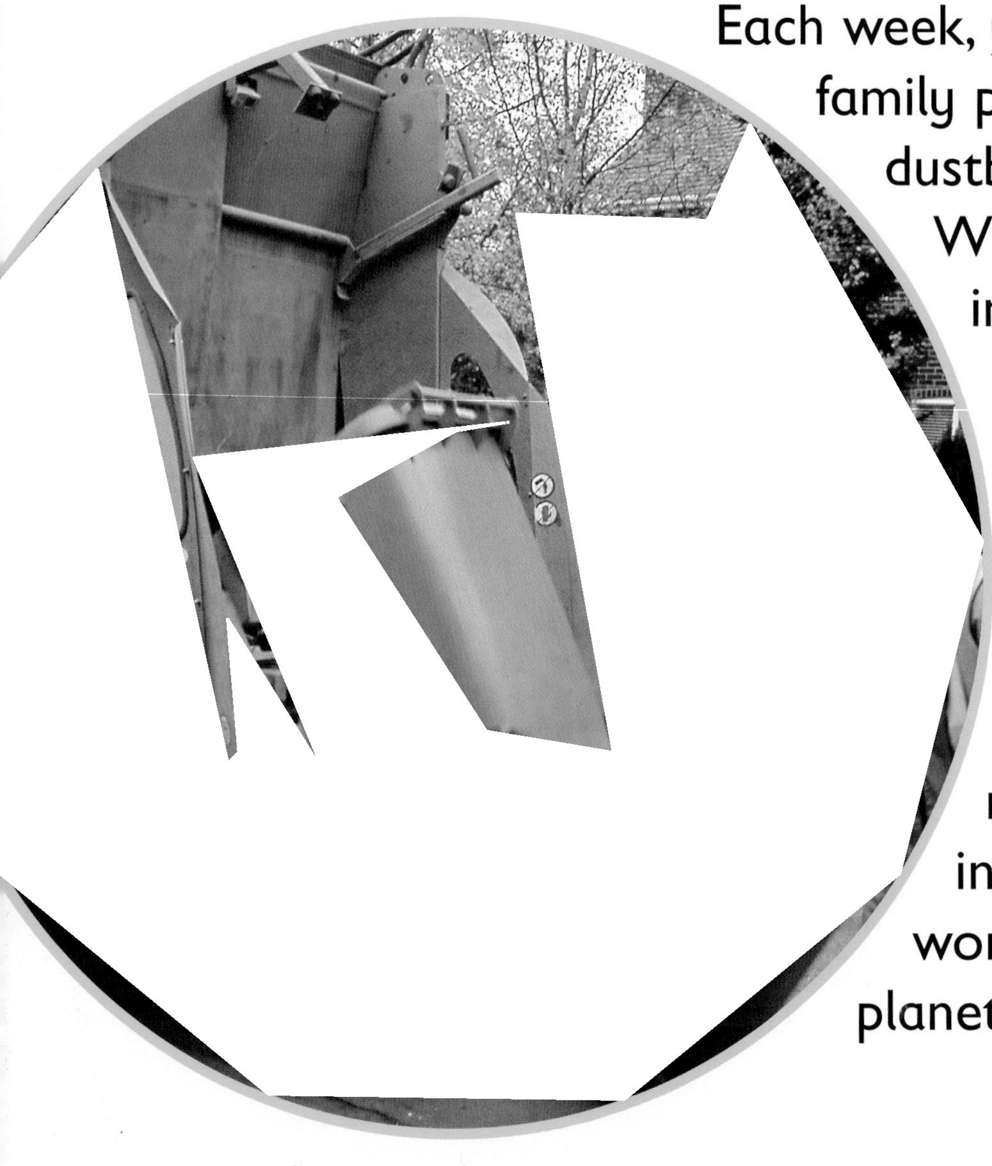

Each week, you and your family produce at least one dustbin full of rubbish. With all the people in the world, that makes a huge amount of waste. Getting rid of rubbish is a problem. It is building up in rubbish tips and in the natural world to harm our planet and its wildlife.

▲ *In many countries, rubbish is collected each week by truck.*

We can all help to solve the problem of rubbish by following the three R's – **reduce**, **reuse** and **recycle**. Reducing means using less of something. Reusing means using something again. Recycling is when rubbish is used to make a new product.

The number of people in the world is growing. More people make more rubbish, so the problem of getting rid of waste is getting bigger, too!

▶ *Rubbish contains useful* **materials** *that can be recycled.*

What's in the bin?

Have you ever thought about what goes in your dustbin? Every week, people throw away newspapers, magazines and leftover food. Some people also put tins, glass bottles, plastic containers, old clothes, toys and worn out machinery in the bin.

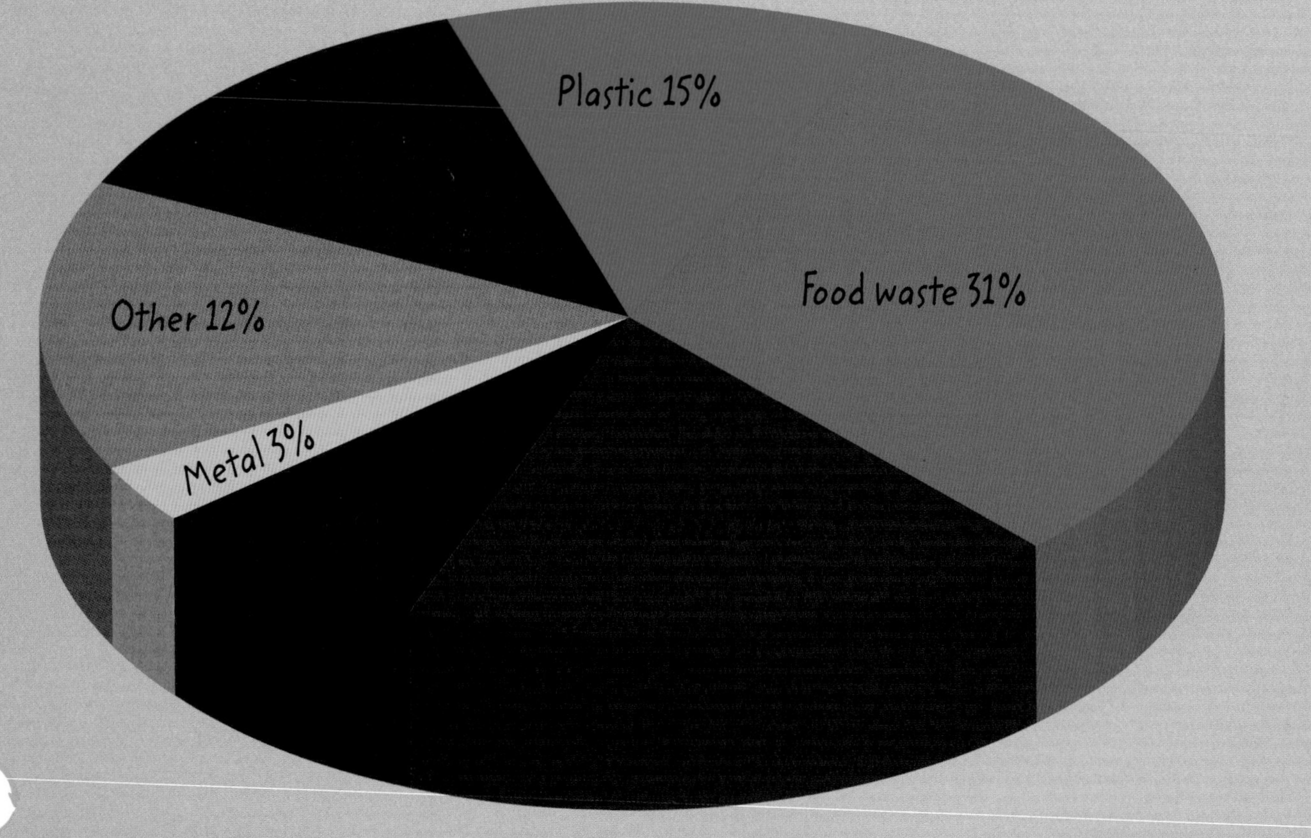

▼ *This pie chart shows the amounts of different sorts of rubbish we threw away in Britain, in 2008.*

▶ **Fast food** *such as pizza comes with a lot of packaging, which is often just thrown away.*

You Can Help!

Find out how much waste your family throws away each week. Make a chart with headings such as 'Food waste' and 'Plastic'. Keep a record of what items are thrown away. Are you able to reduce the amount of rubbish?

A lot of what we throw away is packaging – the wrappings of the things we buy. Packaging can help to protect things, but often it just makes them look bright and colourful. Packaging is made from materials such as paper, card and plastic that could be reused.

Mountains of rubbish

All the rubbish we throw away has to be put somewhere. A lot gets dumped in **landfill sites**. Some is burned in very hot **furnaces** called **incinerators**. But gases from these furnaces can **pollute** the air.

◀ *A truck dumps waste at a landfill site. Sometimes waste leaks out of the dump to pollute the air, water or soil.*

Did You Know?

People in different countries produce different amounts of rubbish. A family in the United States of America (USA) makes seven times as much rubbish as a family in India.

Rubbish dumped in landfill sites is squashed and buried. In the end the landfill site gets full. Many countries are running out of places to put these dumps. Some rubbish is dumped at sea, where it can harm wildlife.

◀ *At the shops, choose products with less packaging. That way, there is less rubbish to throw away.*

A lot of litter

Litter is rubbish that gets dropped instead of being put in a bin. Litter clutters cities and spoils the beauty of the countryside. It can also harm wildlife. For example, animals such as birds and seals can die if they swallow or get tangled up in plastic.

◀ *Dumped litter spoils the look of the countryside.*

◀ *Animals such as this hedgehog can get trapped in the plastic rings used to hold drinks cans.*

LITTER SURVEY

1. Find a place near you where litter is a problem – for example, your school grounds or a park.
2. What types of litter have been left – is it paper, food waste, packaging or dumped machinery?
3. Make a chart with headings such as 'Food Waste,' 'Plastic' and 'Packaging.' You could send your chart to your local **council** and ask them to organise a clean up.

You Can Help!

Ask your teacher to organise a class trip to clean up a local park or beauty spot. Remember to wear gloves.

Will it rot?

Some kinds of rubbish **rot** more quickly than others. **Natural** materials such as food, paper and garden waste rot quite quickly. Fruit and vegetables can be recycled on the **compost** heap. They make a good **fertiliser** for the garden.

▶ *These fruit and vegetable peelings have started to rot in just a few days.*

Paper takes about a month to rot. Wool and cloth take about a year. Tin cans take about 300 years, plastic about 450 years. Glass does not rot.

Man-made materials such as plastic, glass and metal take longer to **decay**. If they are dropped on the ground they will stay the same for hundreds of years.

▼ *Plastic, metal and glass last a long time, harming the natural world.*

Reduce, reuse, recycle

Everyone can help to solve the problem of waste. The first thing to do is to reduce the amount of rubbish you throw away. Can you share or borrow things instead of buying them? Reuse paper, glass jars and plastic bags. Can broken things be mended?

▶ *In some countries, such as Tunisia, people repair things rather than throw them away.*

Recycling is when glass, metal and other materials are saved and used either to make the same thing or something new. In some areas the council collects materials for recycling from homes. In other places we can take them to a **recycling bank**.

▶Look out for these symbols to help you decide what to do with your rubbish.

You Can Help!

Separate materials for recycling such as glass, paper and plastic. Rinse containers to make sure they are clean.

Bottles and jars

Every family in Britain throws away at least one glass bottle or jar a week. Glass can be recycled. It can also be reused, for example, old bottles can hold candles or flowers. Jam jars make great pencil pots!

◀ *Different colours of glass go into different banks. Never throw glass. Just place it gently in the bin.*

◀ *These bottles are waiting to be recycled.*

Glass is made by heating sand and **limestone** in a furnace at a very high temperature. This uses a lot of **energy**. Glass can easily be recycled. Bottles and jars are crushed and reheated at a lower temperature to make new glass. Recycling glass saves energy and **raw** materials.

Making recycled glass uses less energy than making fresh glass. In some countries, such as Sweden, people often return glass bottles to be refilled.

Tins and cans

Tins are made of a material called steel. Drinks cans are made from aluminium. These metals are made from **minerals** dug from the ground and heated in a furnace. This uses up a lot of energy and causes **pollution**.

▶ *Tins and cans can be squashed using a tin can crusher, before taking them to a recycling bank.*

Tins and cans are difficult to reuse, but they are easy to recycle. The used tins and cans are reheated, melted and moulded to make new ones. Recycling tins and cans saves energy and cuts pollution.

▶ *Most of the tins and cans you see in supermarkets contain some recycled metal.*

Paper and card

We throw away a lot of paper and card each week. This includes newspapers, post, books and a lot of packaging. Paper and card are made from wood **pulp**, which is made from trees. Paper and card are easy to recycle.

◀ *Used newspaper can be shredded and mixed with water to make a mushy pulp. This is rolled thin to make recycled paper.*

Making five tonnes of recycled paper (this is the same weight as an elephant) can save up to 85 trees.

TIPS FOR REDUCING WASTE AND REUSING PAPER

1. You can reduce paper waste by asking the post office to stop delivering **junk mail** to your home.
2. Use both sides of paper to write on. Print on both sides of the paper, too.
3. Reuse old envelopes using sticky tape.
4. You can also reuse wrapping paper if you open your presents carefully.

▼ *You can recycle old birthday and Christmas cards to make great gift tags!*

The problem with plastic

Toys, clothes, packaging and cars can be made using plastic. So can glue, paint and carrier bags. There are many types of plastic, such as nylon which is used in clothing, and polystyrene, used in foam packaging. All are made from oil using a lot of energy.

◀ *Buy one large plastic drinks bottle and refill it instead of buying lots of small ones.*

Plastic is light and strong but it rots very slowly, which makes it a problem to get rid of. When it is burned it can give off a **poisonous** gas. Plastic can be recycled to make all sorts of useful things, from fleece jackets and sleeping bags to crates and furniture. You can also reuse plastic pots and tubs as containers.

▶ *This fleece has been made from recycled plastic.*

We use 20 times more plastic today as people did 50 years ago.

Dealing with plastic

Recycling plastic is expensive because the many different types all have to be sorted and recycled separately. For this reason, it is better to reduce the amount of plastic you waste. You can also reuse plastic. For example, reuse plastic bags when you go shopping.

◀ *Take a cloth bag when you go shopping, so you don't need plastic bags at all.*

TIPS FOR REDUCING PLASTIC WASTE

1. Choose food in paper cartons or glass bottles rather than plastic containers.
2. Avoid using plastic plates, cups and cutlery. Use ordinary ones that can be washed and used again.

▼ *You can buy unpackaged fruit and vegetables at a market.*

Clothes, toys and machinery

People have always bought clothes as new styles come into fashion. Nowadays we also want new mobile phones and computers, and the latest toys and games. We sometimes throw away old things that could still be used. Old clothes, books and toys can all be sold, for example at **charity shops**.

◀ *Charity shops sell second-hand clothes and books to raise money for people in need.*

▶ *Car boot fairs are great places to sell any unwanted items.*

REUSING AND RECYCLING

1. Ask your family to find out if faulty machinery can be repaired rather than thrown away.
2. Some shops that sell mobile phones will take your old one to be reused or recycled.
3. Organise a 'swap shop' at school to sell your stuff and get new things.
4. You could sell any unwanted items at a boot fair or give them to a jumble sale.

Start a compost heap

Start a compost heap for food waste and garden trimmings. Putting compost on the garden helps plants and vegetables grow strong and healthy.

YOU WILL NEED:

- an ice cream tub,
- a sponge,
- a compost heap or bin outside – you can buy a plastic compost bin from your local council or garden centre.

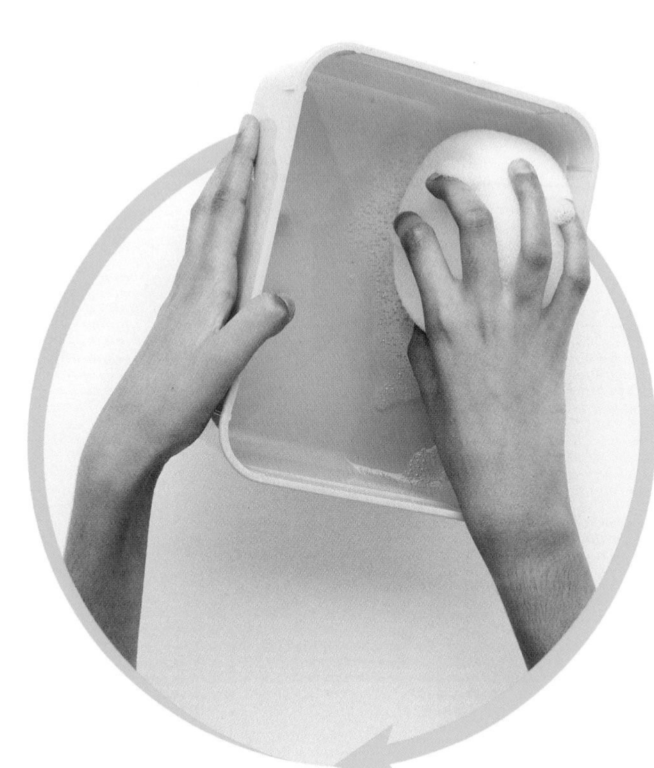

1. Reuse an old ice cream tub. Wash it using washing-up liquid.

2. Wearing gloves, sort out your rubbish. Dead flowers, fruit and vegetable peelings, garden waste and shredded paper can all be put on the compost heap. Don't put meat scraps or cooked food on the heap.

3. Put the sorted rubbish into your ice cream tub. Replace the lid.

4. When the tub is full ask an adult to tip the contents onto the compost heap or bin outside.

5. In three months time, hey presto! Rich compost will be ready to put on your garden.

Further information

Topic map

GEOGRAPHY

Contact your council to find out the location of local landfill sites and recycling centres. Look them up on a map.

SCIENCE

Use a magnet to check whether tins and cans are made from steel or aluminium. Steel is magnetic, aluminium is not.

ART/DESIGN

Toilet rolls and plastic tubs and trays can be used in craft projects. Use shredded paper to make papier mâché to mould figures and masks.

ENGLISH

Write a report on why it's important to reduce, reuse and recycle. Or write a story about recycling from the point of view of a glass bottle or drinks can!

HISTORY

Find out when paper, glass, steel and plastic were first invented using the Internet or a local library.

MATHS

Sell some items at a jumble sale. Put price labels on your things, and make sure you give people the right change. Add up all the money you make at the sale.

Further reading

Environment Action: Recycle by Kay Barnham (Wayland, 2008)
Green Team: Waste and Recycling by Sally Morgan (Franklin Watts, 2008)
Improving Our Environment: Waste and Recycling by Carol Inskipp (Wayland, 2005)
Making a Difference: Reducing Rubbish by Sue Barraclough (Franklin Watts, 2006)

Websites

www.epa.gov/kids/garbage.htm
Information for children on recycling and dealing with waste in the US.

http://earth911.org/
Information for children on how to reduce, reuse and recycle waste.

www.defra.gov.uk/ENVIRONMENT/WASTE/
Information about the problem of waste in the UK.

www.wastewatch.org.uk
Tips on how to reduce waste.

www.wasteonline.org.uk/
Incredible facts about rubbish.

www.olliesworld.com/aus/html/reduce_waste.html
This website, especially for children, offers information on recycling in the US, Australia and the UK.

Glossary

charity shop a shop that sells second-hand items to raise money for a good cause

compost natural materials, which rot to make fertiliser for plants

council the organisation that runs services such as waste collection in your area

decay to rot or to go bad

energy the power to do work

fast food ready-made food, which you can buy and eat straight away

fertiliser a substance added to the soil to make plants grow more easily

furnace a hot oven in which things are burned

incinerator a very hot furnace in which rubbish is burned

junk mail post that is delivered to many homes to advertise businesses

landfill site a rubbish dump, where waste is buried underground

limestone a rock which is used to make glass

man-made something made that is not found naturally

material something used to make something else

mineral a non-living natural substance

natural something that is found naturally

poisonous a substance that can make you ill if you swallow or sometimes touch it

pollute when harmful materials dirty the air, water or soil

pollution when harmful material gets into the air, water or soil

pulp a mushy mixture

raw a natural material such as wood

recycle when rubbish is saved and remade into a new product

recycling bank a centre where waste materials are recycled

reduce to make something smaller or use less of it

reuse when something is used again

rot when a substance breaks down

Index

Numbers in **bold** refer to a photograph.